PERSONAL PAPARAZZI

YOUR BRAND STORY TOLD YOUR WAY

ALINA VINCENT AND CHRISTINE WHITMARSH

PUBLISHED BY BUSINESS PUBLICATIONS PRESS

Published by Business Publications Press
59 Damonte Ranch Parkway
Suite B301
Reno NV 89521 USA
adryenn@wowisme.net
http://wowisme.net

Printed in the United States of America.

First Edition

"The way to gain a good reputation is to endeavor to be what you desire to appear."
-*Socrates*

Acknowledgments

The authors wish to thank:

Adryenn Ashley, inspiration advisor extraordinaire!

Ken Kragen, for his mentorship, a thoughtful book foreword, and his overall support of the project.

Fellow members of our local eWomen Network chapter in Reno for their incredible entrepreneurial support, and for letting us bounce ideas off them.

Our clients, for trusting us with the telling of their brand stories.

Alexios Saskalidis for patiently designing a book cover with paparazzi pizazz!

The team at Christine, Ink for their editorial support.

All our Mikes and the kids… two and four legged.

CONTENTS

FOREWORD

Here it is, a totally readable, wonderfully informative and delightfully enjoyable book that can make a major difference for you and the way you market yourself and your brand.

The thing that you need to understand is that success in any business or personal endeavor depends first on getting attention and that depends in large part on creating your own form of celebrity and developing your own unique story.

Seasoned professionals, Alina Vincent and Christine Whitmarsh will show you how to do that without sacrificing your integrity or that of your business.

Using show business analogies to keep things lively and interesting Alina and Christine have filled this book with simple, effective ways to get to the heart of your story and deliver it to your audience.

In my decades-long career working in Hollywood, I have seen first-hand the effect of crafting a compelling story that really connects with an audience emotionally. In Personal Paparazzi, you will learn how to do the same in your business.

Using some proven techniques that have been around for years and new technology that is changing rapidly, but allows far greater outreach than ever before, these women show you how to stay on the cutting edge of the game and reap the benefits that come from being there.

For years I've personally taught corporations, executives and students how to apply the same concepts to their own lives and businesses that I've used to build the careers of superstars such as Kenny Rogers, Lionel Richie,

Trisha Yearwood and many others. The fact is these things are not limited to the entertainment field, they're relevant to anyone in any line of work.

Alina and Christine understand this and lay it all out for you. Having them on your "team" is a huge first step to increase your success. Enjoy their book and apply their ideas and you'll have terrific results.

Ken Kragen

Ken Kragen,
Celebrity Manager and Organizer of "We Are the World" and "Hands Across America"
http://KenKragen.com

INTRODUCTION

You might be a bit puzzled as you are looking at this book, wondering what the Hollywood paparazzi have to do with you as a business owner. Fear not – this book is not about the latest celebrity gossip. Instead we will focus on ways you can make your **business** a celebrity.

In *Personal Paparazzi*, you will learn the secret to positioning yourself and rising above your competition in a noisy digital world with continuously evolving marketing platforms. You will discover how to create strong long-lasting connections with your customers and create a strong brand image protected from minor missteps!

Savvy celebrities use the paparazzi to spin their story their way and build industry buzz around their name. Savvy entrepreneurs, in order to succeed in the digital marketplace today, must do the same! This book will focus on a **deliberate strategy** that the most successful marketing, branding and publicity pros are using to tell their stories, charm their audiences, and create irresistible brands.

Staying ahead of the curve requires a clear strategy for achieving visibility, recognition, and exposure. If you are using marketing methods from yesterday, you are already behind. The world is changing at an astounding rate. Everything from social media, to digital advertising, to the mobile world, to technology advances is evolving daily. And it's not only the technology; consumers are changing as well. How they are spending money, where they are looking for products and services, how they consume content, what they are expecting—everything is changing. If you are not adapting and adjusting the way you are doing business—don't be surprised when your competition leaves you in the dust!

So, you need to ask yourself right now—is your business in the spotlight or in the wings? Are your customers your loyal screaming fans? Are you attracting the right premium clients that are ready to open their wallets for you? If not—the ideas and strategies in this book might be just the right **secret weapon** that you can use to control your brand narrative, align with your customers, and get the edge over your competition!

Get answers to these questions and more:

1.   Your customers are talking about you at this very minute. How can you find out what they are saying (and then do something about it if you don't like it)?

2.   The days of "set it and forget it" marketing are over. What is the new best practice and how can you implement it in your business?

3.   Is your reputation positive, negative, or worse—completely invisible? What is the correct strategy to use for each type of reputation?

4.   What is *the* hottest way of communicating information in marketing today (Hint: it's connected directly to psychology and emotion!) and how can you utilize it?

Are you ready to get started?

Note: Because the digital marketplace is changing daily, and new apps and platforms are constantly being created and introduced, we tried to avoid details and specific recommendations in this book. For up-to-date information on the topics covered, visit our blogs:

For words: http://Christine-Ink.com/christines-ink

For images: http://AlinaVincentPhotography.com/Blog

Thank you for purchasing our book!

Join our mailing list and get updates on new releases, branding advice, visual and written marketing strategies, and other great content.

Click here to sign up: http://Personal-Paparazzi.com/Newsletter

1

TABLOID TRUTHS

The glare of the celebrity spotlight is intense, especially when paparazzi are involved. In fact, doing something as simple as having dinner at an L.A. hotspot like Spago can be dangerous to the senses. A celebrity (along with any unfortunate bystanders) can be subjected to temporary blindness from the glare of simultaneous flashbulbs, and temporary deafness from the mass shouting of his or her name. Jealous? Probably not. This, along with other less than flattering paparazzi perceptions such as car chases down Sunset Blvd., and photographers scaling the walls of private properties, going through the trash, and invading the privacy of the star and their family, is enough to put a damper on anyone's Hollywood daydreams. To be clear, this is the dark side of the paparazzi, the area of crossed ethical and legal boundaries. This is not what this book is about. Law breaking aside, many celebrities, while acknowledging that the paparazzi can often be intrusive, understand that the publicity they generate can be a game changer in the battle between becoming yesterday's news or today's hottest headline.

If you think about it, the paparazzi are persistent, constant, on-scene storytellers, tying together a celebrity's personal and professional images. They have the power to reveal so many authentic angles of who this "star" really is, thus increasing rapport with their fans, that more than a few famous people have been known to HIRE their services. Even the celebrities who choose not to go to such lengths are keenly aware of how "the game" works. For instance, if you are the star of a brand new, multi-million dollar summer blockbuster and your agent tells you to increase buzz for the movie by "being seen," would it be wiser to hide out in your sweats at home, or to dress up, call up one of your co-stars from the movie, and head to a Sunset Strip hotspot for a publicized night out on the town?

Or think about another personal plotline that a star would love for their fans to read about—redemption. Sure a celebrity might mess up and end up in trouble, but then, months later the paparazzi may be snapping pictures of him or her giving back to the community, laughing with friends and enjoying a clean, healthy life. The paparazzi, love 'em or hate 'em, hold immense power amidst their frantically snapping shutters to add depth, value, and even longevity to a celebrity's brand image.

So, were you jealous of the star being pursued by paparazzi as he or she left Spago? Well, maybe you should be! Just how much publicity is your business getting right now? Are customers chasing you down the sidewalk begging to buy from you? Imagine if your products and services were in such high demand. How great would that be?

But that's not all. *Right now* and you may not even be aware of it, someone, somewhere, is talking about you. In Hollywood this is called gossip and is the stuff of supermarket tabloids. And what is gossip? It's when someone talks behind your back about your business. But let's pause for a second – what if "your business" is actually YOUR BUSINESS?!

In the business world, gossip comes in the form of private conversations based on customer experience, user reviews on sites like Yelp, outdated, unflattering photos of you from ten years ago still ranked high by Google, social media conversations that you participated in, and even snapshots of your products and services on Instagram.

We all know how bad reviews can hurt businesses and turn hundreds of clients away. If you are searching for a nice hotel for your trip, a single review about dirty sheets might send you elsewhere, right? And what if it's accompanied by pictures as well? Even if that same hotel has hundreds of other positive comments you'll think – "Dirty sheets? Yuck!" When the impact of such negative reviews reaches a certain tipping point, it can actually be damaging enough to shut down the business.

So let's get something straight right now – if you are in business, you already have paparazzi. The worst kind, too – the invisible kind! Everybody who has ever come in contact with you, used your services or products, or even heard something about you from their friends, is out there telling your story. Gossip is what everyone's saying about you when you're not around. The question you need to ask yourself is: *Do I want my brand impression to be controlled by gossip, or do I want to control my own narrative and tell my brand story my way?*

Beyond simply revealing the *truth* about your brand, if you are in business today in the age of social media and expected transparency, you have a unique opportunity – and obligation – to reveal the real *person* behind your brand, your "authentic you." The celebrities as well as the photographers who follow them have also realized this. Have you noticed how the days of snapping the most scandalous, unflattering pictures of stars for the highest paparazzi price tag are largely behind us? The trend now is – "stars are just like us." Photographers are now rewarded for snapping images of celebrities that help their fans relate to them, and thus trust them, and thus watch their movies and TV shows. The same is true for business. Your customers want to know, connect with, and then buy from the human being behind products and services. Don't put forward an image that you think your audience would like to see, give them the real deal. If you are not authentic in your messaging, people will see right through it. Nobody wants perfect anymore. Perfect is not authentic and can even be seen as less trustworthy. The world is hungry for real. No one wants to see a pristine office environment: they'd rather see a working desk with stacks of papers because they can relate to that. Nobody wants to see a perfectly styled burger in a laboratory-like environment. They want to see a messy stack of beef and fixings with home-made sauce dripping all over it, because it's real and makes their mouth water. Don't post overly enthusiastic clean politically correct social media status updates. Show a bit of your personality and your values, and take a stand once in a while.

Being real doesn't mean that you should use poor quality snapshots, or post blogs and tweets with rampant spelling and grammatical errors. You must have professional photography and proofread your sound bites if you want to appear professional, but the subject itself doesn't have to be picture perfect. From your authentic self to the truth about what it is you're selling, in business today you *must* take charge of your brand story. If you don't show and tell people who you are, what you do, and why it matters, they will decide for themselves – and sometimes, the stories they tell will hurt your business and you will lose money.

When positive, on the other hand, brand exposure and public perception have the power to benefit your business. This is exactly the kind of heightened visibility that is essential to growing your business too. This unique hybrid of marketing, PR, reputation management, and brand thinking is the secret weapon to place you above your competition that most businesses aren't even aware of yet. Everyone needs an edge in business. What you're about to read in this book is intended to give you that competitive advantage.

Now, let's look at the nuts and bolts of this secret weapon, this tactical advantage available to you right now that you can use to surpass your competitors - one that we choose to call Personal Paparazzi. So, what is it and how can it realistically benefit your business?

There are many essential functions in your business – things that need to get done to keep the lights on, the phones ringing, and the money flowing in. It takes tasks like bookkeeping, staffing, administration, and IT to keep the business running. Now consider one of the biggest functions in your business – sales, which means attracting (i.e. marketing to) customers.

Consider Personal Paparazzi to be the newest member of your team, the newest essential sales function of your business. In a sense, it's the missing piece between your message and the ability of your audience to resonate with it. For the purposes of this book, when we refer to "your Personal Paparazzi," we're talking about this new entity (brought to life by either you, your team, or outside professionals) that strategically and consistently produces the abundance of high quality words and images that you need to tell the complete brand story, required to connect with audiences in today's world.

Because times have changed and, therefore, you must change the way you reach your customers. Are you still marketing to your customers today the same way that you (and others) did a few years ago? You may not realize it yet, but the world has changed around you. As evidence of this, take an honest look at your business and ask – are you growing as fast as you always have and as much as you want to? Are you attracting customers as easily as you used to? When it comes to your marketing methods, you've probably been doing what you've been doing for years. But recently, and maybe you can't even put your finger on why, something has changed. The quality of results you're seeing based on the efforts and money invested, are out of sync. You're reaching out to your audience the same way you always have, but for some reason they're not hearing you.

Personal Paparazzi: The people who help bring exposure, recognition, and visibility to your brand through the strategic use of words and images.

Conclusion

Storytelling creates emotional connections with your customers. In this new era of marketing, telling the right story and evoking emotions in your customers is what sells. Famed marketer and bestselling author Seth Godin says, "A brand cannot exist unless someone tells themselves a story about what they are buying." Marketing now is about selling an experience, rather than a product or service. Therefore, your Personal Paparazzi can be seen as creative storytellers who can help describe your customers' brand experience using compelling words and images.

In *Personal Paparazzi,* you will see how, in order to create a successful and profitable business you must control your own narrative, by telling your story and creating strong emotional connections with your customers.

2

DAMAGE CONTROL

It's a Hollywood publicist's worst nightmare. Or, more realistically, it's her typical Saturday night. Even before her client, a young up and coming movie star, makes a jailhouse call to his lawyer following his arrest, the publicist is already staring in dismay at the screaming headlines, photos, and incriminating videos on the tabloid news site. She then springs into action, doing "damage control" for the young celeb. Immediately, and in the following weeks, she will flood the Internet with a barrage of positive press – existing images, articles, press releases, and past interviews from her client's content arsenal – to offset the bad publicity. For every bad headline, the publicist knows, she needs at least twenty good ones to minimize the damage. In a relatively short amount of time, that young movie star is once again a media darling, moving beyond the scandal with his reputation restored.

What does this have to do with you and your business? Has your brand image ever suffered from the daggers of competitors, company missteps, unhappy customers, defective products, and other naturally occurring things in business that can tarnish your reputation? Just like a celebrity, your brand is susceptible to bad reviews, corporate scandals, and, as a result, lost customers. You can't just ignore the bad publicity. The story won't go away, it will just go on without you. The solution lies in creating an abundance of positive publicity to counteract the bad! If you are guilty, apologize and make things right. If you are caught in a lie, fess up and move on (the public is far more likely to forgive you if you are being honest). If you are being wrongly accused, tell your side of the story. In addition, flood the digital marketplace and share with your audience the right images, words, and marketing messages that will put you in a good light while pushing the "bad stuff" past the first pages of search engines.

Times are changing. Ten years ago, before the tremendous growth of the Internet, instant access to information, and the explosion of social media, businesses had the luxury of reacting at a slower pace. There was time to deal with a mistake before the whole world found out about it. Now, with immediate access to news, a story can circle the globe before you blink. News of the misstep goes viral and often gets picked up by the media, especially if the message is funny, hurtful, or otherwise controversial. Unfortunately, the media thrives on controversy and, if we're being honest, failure and negativity. When a brand messes up the media can't wait to fan the flames.

The good news is that as a business owner you also have tools at your disposal to establish (or repair) your reputation and restore trust in your brand. With the right strategy in place, you can counteract and diminish any scandal or bad publicity by taking advantage of the instant access to online distribution platforms. And the best part? It's free.

Think about Domino's Pizza. For years they were primarily known for their "30 minutes or free" guarantee. Then two Domino's employees made a not very flattering video of Domino's and the video went viral.

Domino's had been using the same pizza recipe for fifty years. Between the viral video and dissatisfied customers, Domino's was at the center of a social media nightmare.

Domino's could have denied the reality of the situation or even gone into hiding, as far as brand publicity was concerned. Instead the company used the tools at their disposal: YouTube, Twitter, Facebook, and launched a new campaign called Domino's Pizza Turnaround—complete with its own website, http://pizzaturnaround.com. Domino's even made a short film on how executives listened to their customers. The Domino's Pizza Turnaround documentary currently has over one and half million views!

Even though the Domino's story appears to have a happy ending, consumers in today's digital world may forgive, but they rarely forget. Despite a company's very best rebranding and publicity efforts, even when the smoke clears, in the age of instant access and bottomless virtual archives, no image, headline, or word is truly ever "gone." What you can do, however, to combat this, is ensure that the bad is buried and the good is displayed on page one. An online marketing expert once said, "The best place to hide a body is on the second page of Google."

Controlling your digital footprint will help you dominate your industry with the good publicity you've generated for your brand image. Incidentally, the reason for our emphasis on your digital brand image throughout this book is that the time and effort required to invest in your digital reputation typically yields a much higher ROI than traditional platforms such as word of mouth, radio/TV, or print media.

If you're a business owner or brand without your own high-paid PR team constantly monitoring your brand image, what can you do to not only fix, but also actually *manage* your reputation? You could of course take your own pictures, write blog posts, and create and distribute press releases. But is that really enough to create a strong enough impression in the midst of the online noise from everyone else trying to do the same exact thing? Sometimes it is, but most of the time it's not. Your message is more likely to get lost in the static, an "extra" in a crowd of hundreds of other background actors. In order to stand out and be a star, you must have a strategy to create and implement powerful written and visual content, purposefully and constantly.

In addition to having a strategy, you must also have the time to execute it. Yes, you may have the skills to regularly create quality content, but do you have the time? Most business owners simply can't take precious resources away from running and growing the business to become the brand's publicist, writer, and photographer. It's really not high on their list of priorities. When you pull back and look at the big picture of everything your business needs, in relation to your greatest strengths, is it the best decision for you to take on these roles?

The ability to promote your business with words and images is absolutely essential to the telling of a complete, compelling, and engaging brand story that attracts ready-to-buy clients. So what is the solution? How do you get the job done?

Imagine your own Personal Paparazzi, the newest member of your team and your new secret weapon. Your Personal Paparazzi is your team of experts whose only job is to promote you at your brand best to your target market. Just like some celebrities have personal chefs, stylists, or chauffeurs, your Personal Paparazzi is your tailored service that helps you promote your business through targeted content. This team of experts works diligently, continuously generating original words and images of the highest quality, so that you can tell your story in a way that creates an emotional connection with your audience. You can then use this content to show up online, putting you in control of your narrative in the process. With your own Personal Paparazzi you can be in total control of the story being told to the world, setting the right expectations and attracting your ideal paying clients.

By taking control of your story you place yourself in a position of power. You are no longer working from a reactive place, constantly fighting fires and doing damage control. Instead, you are proactively building your reputation through quality words and images that tell your brand story your way. Your Personal Paparazzi content creation team takes the time to understand your business, your message, and your goals. They analyze your current position in the world, align it with your target, and as a result, create a personalized strategy for putting your brand in the spotlight.

Establishing this type of positive, consistent message, communicated across all of your distribution platforms, will create a resilient brand. People do business with people they know, like, and trust. When people are connected to you emotionally they're less likely to believe everything they hear from your competitors and more likely to become your loyal advocates. This kind of relationship doesn't happen overnight, but is built over time. Once you have the trust, once you have built your reputation, if an unexpected negative situation arises, and it will, something that may be a tidal wave for your competitor will be nothing but a small, forgettable ripple for you.

Let's go back to that young celebrity from the beginning of the chapter and his unfortunate evening. His story had a happy ending, which means he most likely had an established good reputation. However, if this incident had been just another in a series of bad publicity, it could have led to a much more damaging outcome, like losing the lead role in a hit TV show. Trying to restore a good reputation after something bad happens is much harder if you didn't have a good reputation to begin with. However, if there was a multitude of positive press released prior to the event then this one unfortunate incident could easily have become a forgettable moment.

As a business owner, you have the power to control the narrative that your existing and potential customers – your fans – hear about you. Is the volume of high quality, positive, purposeful content and the story that you've crafted around your brand great enough to withstand a PR storm?

Conclusion

Now you have learned one key benefit of this new function of your business that we're calling Personal Paparazzi – damage control. By creating and flooding the web with a constant flow of high quality content, when publicity problems do arise, the "good" stuff out there about your brand will vastly outnumber the "bad" stuff. In today's instant information access digital world, it is essential to have this function in place to maintain your strong, positive reputation. Let's take a look at another way that your Personal Paparazzi can benefit your business – brand visibility and reputation.

3

THE GOOD, THE BAD, AND THE UGLY

It's Friday evening and you and your friends are poring through movie reviews, debating which film would be worth shelling out your hard earned dollars. Your debate quickly moves from plotline to the actors starring in the film. Who's hot, who's not, and who you've never heard of. Whether you know it or not, what you're actually debating is which actor's brand is the strongest, strong enough to close the sale at the ticket window.

Once the movie choice is decided, you and your friends move onto another buying decision – the restaurant where you eat dinner before the movie. You all agree that you want to try a new spot, another brand discussion ensues and you are down to three choices. You then do a quick online search for each restaurant. One restaurant has an eye catching, easy to navigate website with crisp, vibrant, professional images of their food, dining room, bar and a welcoming picture of the owner himself. You find your mouth watering just looking at the photos of their dishes! One of your friends hops over to Yelp and is instantly hit with a number of glowing reviews for the restaurant. Then, you locate the restaurant on Facebook and

"LIKE" it. You notice on their social media networks how engaged they are, posting several times a day with strongly worded calls to action and photos of their daily specials. They also take the time to engage with their enthusiastic fans, responding to their comments and questions and thanking them for visiting the restaurant and sharing content from the page with their friends.

The remaining restaurants are deemed not as hot by the group; one has an uninspiring website with dark snapshots of the food and menu items listed with no descriptions. Yelp reviews reveal that while the drink menu is good and the servers go above and beyond, the food quality is poor and the overall dining experience lackluster. They have a mostly empty Facebook page created a few years ago, with the last post dated over six months ago.

Finally, the third restaurant to be discussed fares worst of all in the online visibility contest. It has no website (or one that you can't find in the first few pages of Google search results), no digital content such as blogs and social media pages, and zero consumer reviews. It might as well be non-existent. Even though one of you saw it driving by and thought of checking it out, this choice is quickly abandoned because you can't find anything online that supports it. So, when it comes down to the decision, it's not hard to see which restaurant you and your friends are most likely to go to. The first one with the obvious effort made to promote its brand ("the good"), the second one with some good points but mostly bad ("the bad"), or the third, mostly invisible one ("the ugly")?

Newsflash: if this is how you make your buying decisions, it's likely that your customers choose the same way! Therefore, the same theory of "good, bad and ugly" applies to your brand reputation. A brand with a good reputation is visible, easily recognizable, has positive buzz around it, purposefully creates and shares quality brand content, and is consistent in its messaging, tone, and style. A brand with a bad reputation is also recognizable. However, the overall brand impression is generally more negative than positive.

You might think there's nothing worse than having a bad reputation. But the truth is, not being visible in the marketplace to your customers in today's digital marketplace is actually hurting your brand more. When your potential customers can't find you online, that's an ugly way of doing business!

How many business owners have, with the very best of intentions, put forth the time and effort to create a Facebook fan page, a Twitter account, a LinkedIn profile, or a Pinterest page, only to later abandon those pages? You might be invisible because you don't have time to maintain an online presence, you're not tech savvy, or simply because you are just starting out, rebranding or changing the name or the scope of your business. Invisible is ugly, but it is also redeemable and fixable. Businesses who have an invisible brand can benefit immensely from putting time and effort into creating a digital story around their brand or by having their own Personal Paparazzi.

Do you know where your brand falls on the "good, bad, and ugly" spectrum? It's important to know this because where you fall might not only be costing you customers, but can also foreshadow potential consequences when the unexpected strikes. As we saw, there are three stops on this spectrum of public opinion. First, there is "ugly", when you have no reputation at all therefore, one bad review can be the death of your brand as far as publicity is concerned. When you have a "bad" reputation, one additional unfavorable review is more likely to blend in with other bad and mediocre reviews, and cause less of a ripple in your reputation. Finally and ideally, when you have a good reputation, even a mix of bad and good will generally tilt in the favor of good. Even several bad reviews will not do much to sway the opinion of the public if you have a strong positive foundation.

Whether your brand is currently being perceived as good, bad, or ugly, who is creating the narrative of that image? Perhaps you have already contracted professionals to tell your brand story through high quality words and images. Or maybe you and your employees occasionally remember to do a "drive by," tossing up some content for the sake of doing "something" (versus nothing). Or, in the ugliest of scenarios - perhaps you don't have an online image to maintain at all! If you're like most busy business owners, your online image is something you probably haven't given much thought to. You may know it exists; perhaps you Google yourself once in a while out of curiosity. But largely, it's something that's not very high on your daily list of tasks and priorities.

How likely are your customers to buy from you based on the results of their online, word of mouth, and media research? Reality check: as you're reading this now, somebody somewhere who is considering doing business with you is "Googling" you and your business and making a buying decision based on the images and words that come up. With the simple click of a button, your prospective customers are mentally labeling you as "good," bad," or "ugly." As they do so, they are asking themselves: Who is this? What's their story? Why should I spend money with them? Or that classic business question – what's in it for me?

Before you can adjust your brand story to effectively answer these questions and make a strong argument to your customers, you must find out what needs to be fixed. One way to find out how you are "showing up" to your audience is by performing a digital inventory on your current online reputation. In short, this process entails first putting yourself in your customers' shoes and then searching for yourself to find out what's out there about your brand.

Points to Ponder:

❋ How many times do you show up in the search results?
❋ How high in the results?
❋ Do you like how you show up?
❋ Is the information accurate, timely, abundant, and flattering?
❋ Would YOU buy from you?

Search your competition, compare their results to your own and ask, "who would you buy from if faced with this comparison of brand images?" There is, of course, a far more detailed process of doing a comprehensive digital discovery and truly getting all the information you need to create a brand strategy that will achieve your goals.

For some tips on how to improve your online visual reputation, click here:

http://AlinaVincentPhotography.com/vr/

Set up an early warning system, like Google Alerts, using your own name and your company name, so that when something new shows up online, good or bad, you're the first to know. And that's only the beginning when it comes to social media analytics. What if you knew that there were tons of people, a.k.a. potential customers, having a live conversation about your products and services? Wouldn't you want to know what they were saying about you right now? Of course you would. Social media analytics, also called monitoring, listening, or data mining, is a great way to accomplish this. What this means for your business is finding out what brand message you are transmitting from your business and what people are saying about you so you can fine-tune it to connect better with your audience.

Discovering what your message sounds like in the world, what your audience is saying about you, and seeing the overall impression of your brand, is critical to your business success. Through "listening," you can see mentions of your name, your business name, your products, and your services. You can also monitor what people are saying about your competition (so you can do right what they're perhaps doing wrong), discover additional ways to differentiate your brand from theirs, or convert a new customer.

Many savvy companies use Twitter to listen for negative mentions of their competition and instantly reach out to the customer, showing they care, they are listening and they are the better choice of brand. Through listening, you can be much more reactive to negative feedback from your own customers and minimize the damage by offering a timely response, while also rewarding positive feedback from your biggest fans! The list of all the different sites that fall under the category of social media analytics could easily fill pages. It could also be outdated by the time you read this book. Therefore, we are not going into specific details here. You can, however, download our free report with a list of social media "listening" sites: http://Personal-Paparazzi.com/Monitoring

Having clarity on how you are being seen and what adjustments need to be made to your brand image is powerful for companies and brands of all sizes. Some of the biggest brands in the world have been blindsided when how they *thought* their customers saw them, didn't match their how their customers *actually* saw them. We mentioned earlier how Domino's Pizza was faced with the challenge of reversing their bad reputation as far as the quality of their food was concerned. This story is also a great example of what can happen when what a brand *thinks* their customers think is actually not accurate at all.

Each year, the 'Marketing/Leger Corporate Reputation' Survey grades well-known brands based on percentage of positive public opinions and percentage of negative opinions. For a few years now, the Heinz brand (think ketchup…. or catsup, depending on your preference) has hovered near the top of the leaderboard of most favorably perceived brands. Here's a snapshot of why Heinz keeps coming up on top. When you look at their social media, you see them playing by a unique set of rules native to each platform. For instance, on Twitter, this company is engaging with fans and retweeting, including sharing images of enthusiastic fans alongside their favorite Heinz product. They're also well known for their charitable deeds, giving back to the United Way and various other organizations.

At a different point of the "good, bad and ugly" spectrum, let's look at one example of a well-known brand that found itself labeled as "bad" by many of their customers. In the past few years, Carnival Cruise Lines has experienced power, plumbing, and other various mechanical issues with not one, not two, not three, but FOUR ships in its fleet. From a PR standpoint, this must seem like a pitching machine that baseball players use to practice their swing. Just when they whack one ball back, they're assaulted with more, each one fired at them faster and faster, with little time to recover in between the hits. This is an example of when the "bad" only gets worse before it has a chance to get better. To recover from such a publicity shipwreck, the keepers of the Carnival brand have likely been tasked with creating an extremely targeted, multi-layered, content and PR strategy. The last thing they need is a PR miss that could make things worse. So what did Carnival do to contain the brand damage? For the most part, the usual – press releases and sound bites communicating their commitment to customer service and everything else that makes people love companies and want to buy from them. Then came the barrage of tweets from the official Carnival Twitter account to reinforce their position: *We know you've heard the bad, but here's why we're good.*

Unfortunately, it may have been too little too late, or perhaps the magnitude of the situation far outweighed options for reputation repair.

The worldwide reaction to Carnival's attempted recovery from their series of PR fiascos was largely #omg #wtf.

So where can you see a brand example of "ugly"? Since ugly is defined in this book as not having any sort of reputation or online presence, you likely would be hard up in finding one. Here's what you can do instead on a smaller scale. Search the names of some local businesses in your area, ones that you frequent or have heard of. Who shows up, with a quality website, images, and other content? Who is invisible? How did this search affect (or not affect) your perceptions of these businesses? How does that compare with your own digital presence?

Did you know?

❋ 7 out of 10 consumers are more likely to use a local business if it has information available on a social media site
❋ 88% of consumers who search for a type of local business on a mobile device call or go to that business within 24 hours
❋ 60% of consumers are more likely to consider or contact a business whose images appear in local search results
❋ 85% of consumers are searching for local businesses online, but 25% of local businesses don't show up in search results

The point is, if you are not on your customers' radar you have a lot of work ahead of you.

The good news for brands of all sizes, from Carnival to that local "invisible" business, is that brand image is fixable! As you'll recall from Chapter 2, a key strategy in fixing and rebuilding your image is to flood the Internet with high quality, positive content on a consistent basis. You have to bury the unwanted search results by flooding the Internet with new content. Don't get the wrong idea – fixing your online image is not a one-time event. It takes a deliberate, strategic plan put into action over the course of months just to see the first results and continuous maintenance and course adjustments over the years.

It's the only way to create (or recreate) the right online image for yourself and your business. It works for a couple of different reasons:

1)   Search engines favor the newest content, considering it most timely and relevant, so any new images and written content you upload will supersede the old, showing up higher in the results.

2)   A majority of your potential clients don't look past the first page in a search.

Your goal is to create and upload enough original content, so that it pushes all of the irrelevant, unwanted results past the first page. If you don't have anything to hide, your goal is to simply generate enough relevant content so that it pushes your competition way down in the searches.

If your brand is nonexistent, it just means that you'll have to double up your efforts just to get on your audience's radar. If your brand is tarnished, a healthy push of positive publicity can elevate you from bad to good. And if you're good already, it's now up to you to maintain that positive online image by continuously creating and executing solid visual and written content strategies. In Hollywood, a director cannot coast for very long on the box office success of his last feature film. Business is also based on "what have you done lately?" and nowhere is that more evident than on the Internet where everything is date stamped, so when you take a hiatus from maintaining your brand presence, the search results reflect it. Constant brand maintenance is an ongoing, mission critical responsibility for any business seeking to continue making sales, and rise above its competitors. There's no such thing as effective "drive by" marketing. Reactive marketing is much less effective than working from a proactive, planned out strategy. Effective marketing, the kind that leads to sales, requires absolute consistency or you risk dropping into brand obscurity and in all probability, business decline and possibly even failure. And yes, these strategies might have worked for you in the past. But in business today, you may already be noticing that doing what you've always done, like ads in the Yellow Pages, is suddenly not yielding the same results anymore. It's not what you're doing it's what you're not doing.

The bottom line is, find out what story your audience is telling about you so that if needed, you can make sure the real story of your brand is told. Consumers today trust peer reviews and recommendations more than any other factor when making a buying decision. It's like the story at the beginning of the chapter, when you and your friends get together and ask the collective question – who do we want to do business with?

Conclusion

Hopefully you have seen so far how important it is in business to be acutely aware of your brand impression. Your brand is a living entity that must be fed, watered, monitored, and showcased at all times. This is why having a team that supports you versus taking you away from the things that you ARE good at, is crucial.

The days of "set it and forget it" in advertising, marketing, and PR are gone. Businesses that used to get away with simply renewing the same print ad, with the same tired image and copy, over and over for years at a time, are getting a rude awakening (from their financials) that this strategy no longer works and … Surprise! It hasn't actually worked for years. You must constantly assess and adjust your strategy while striving to improve the quality and relevance of the words and images that tell your brand story. Business is on a treadmill, constantly moving forward with the changing times, as modern platforms like social media, video, and smart phone applications set new standards for the level of communication that the public expects from the brands they buy from. Keeping up with these ever evolving content requirements is no longer an option or a luxury. It's not a matter of whether you think you can afford it or not. You have to invest in your brand to stay visible and to rise above your competition. It's a necessary cost of doing business. The only question is whether you have the time to do it yourself or if you could use some help or guidance with it.

Visit our website to find out if now is the right time to hire your own Personal Paparazzi: http://Personal-Paparazzi.com/DiscoveryCall

Takeaways:

❋ Celebrities have the paparazzi to craft and tell their story and promote their brand. Businesses need the same advantage!

❋ A Personal Paparazzi is a dedicated team of image and word experts (whether this means you, your employees or outside experts) whose job is to promote you – at your brand best – to your target market.

* If you don't show and tell people who you are, what you do, and why it matters, they will decide for themselves (and you may not like what they come up with).
* You need to create a consistent stream of positive, high quality, purposeful content about your brand to keep your business in the spotlight.
* You must know at any given point what your brand reputation is, and be proactive about fixing it.

To find the gaps in your content inventory that are costing you money, download your free content self-assessment on our website at: http://Personal-Paparazzi.com/Content/

This is the first step to begin to assess and analyze whether your brand is "scandalous or fabulous." Now, let's send your story to a Hollywood script doctor to help make the changes needed to make it ready for production!

4

STORYBOARDING

"The other way to persuade people—and ultimately a much more powerful way—is by uniting an idea with an emotion. The best way to do that is by telling a compelling story."

-Robert McKee, award-winning screenwriter/director

Think of the greatest stories you've ever heard, seen, or read – love stories, comedies, dramas, tales of suspense – the ones that really grabbed your attention, activated your imagination, and perhaps even stuck with you long after the book was closed or movie ended. What did they all have in common? Each one evoked an emotion. It may have scared you, made you laugh, cry, get angry or at the basic level, maybe it simply persuaded you to see the world in a different way. Stories, by design, have persuasion power and believe it or not, it all begins with simple human psychology.

As humans we can't help but pay attention to stories. Stories engage both sides of the brain, blending information with emotion. This is by far the most powerful way to connect with people. Visual stories, in particular, help the brain process information and set the scene before words ever can. Storytelling is the most powerful, persuasive and appealing form of disseminating your content.

In business, storytelling is an essential piece of your content strategy. It persuades customers to see your point of view, experience a compelling brand story and, as a result, buy your product or service. This is even truer for higher end businesses that cater strictly to things that people want, but don't necessarily need. It takes the something extra, the next level of marketing to achieve success in this arena – enter emotion. The persuasion power that comes when you can tell a story that stirs an emotion and creates a sensory experience in your audience can give your brand the winning edge over your competition.

Think about some famous brands that have evoked emotion in the form of powerful storytelling as a way of persuading people to purchase their product. Nike, for instance, sells attitude and empowerment packaged in the form of sneakers. Their advertising is designed to forge an emotional connection with their audience every step of the way. Words and images combine to transport you directly into a scene from one of their commercials—running on damp pavement through a sea of dew covered trees in the silent serenity of early morning, hearing the soft slap of your shoes, seeing the foggy mist of your breath, relishing in the feeling of focus, power and peace in your world without anyone to answer to. The complete sensory experience, created by this powerful combination of words and images, stays with you long after the commercial ends. Then, next time you hear the word Nike or see their products in a store, the experience that comes back to you is automatically woven in with the emotions. You feel focused and powerful and you associate those feelings with the purchase of that pair of running shoes.

There are many other examples of effective brand storytelling that you may also be recalling now. The smell of a cup of Folgers coffee in the morning, the way that Klondike bars transport you to an arctic glacier (can you almost feel the chill?), the "orgasmic" experience of washing your hair with Herbal Essences shampoo, and so on. These brands understand the power of story and have purposefully and strategically employed it to induce emotions in their customers—positive emotions that they hope people will then associate with purchasing and using their products. You have this power too.

As we mentioned earlier, story sells. Marketing today is goal based storytelling rather than "pitching" the customer over and over with hard sell after hard sell, hoping to get the sale. Consumers today want and demand more. They want authenticity and originality; something that captivates their attention and makes them feel something. They want an experience.

This does not mean, however, that telling any old story will work. The story you tell must be true to your brand, and the way in which you tell it must fit into an overall strategy that aligns with your goals. The purpose of strategy is ensuring that your story is seen and heard in the right place, by the right audience, and at the right time. In other words – you have to know where you want to go before embarking on the journey of getting there.

"Would you tell me, please, which way I ought to go from here?"
"That depends a good deal on where you want to get to."
"I don't much care where –"
"Then it doesn't matter which way you go."
-Lewis Carroll, Alice in Wonderland

In Hollywood, the strategy that a director uses to ensure that their initial vision for a film on day one matches the final cut, is called storyboarding. The director and cinematographer will sit down with a specialized illustrator, called a storyboard artist, and essentially map out what they want the movie to look like, shot by shot. Each shot is depicted in a separate drawing. This way, the filmmakers can see each piece of the movie "plan" as well as how all the pieces will fit and flow together in the complete film. This is a key element of any good strategy – the ability to zoom in and see individual steps needed to reach the goal as well as being able to see the big picture. Equipped with a complete illustrated roadmap of the film, the filmmakers can then break down the strategy into smaller, actionable tasks such as camera shot lists (step by step directives of where the camera will be from moment to moment in each scene). This way, nothing is left to chance when it comes to the long and winding road from vision to completed product.

Your Personal Paparazzi should have the ability to adopt this planning mentality and craft stories that evoke emotions in your audience, persuading people to buy AND doing it within the construct of a strategy that is aligned with your goals.

Taking the time to sit down and plan the strategic creation of content and images is absolutely necessary if you want the outcome of your branding to match your vision. When businesses choose the "wing it" approach, the quality of their brand story reflects it, and so do their sales. Filmmakers understand this and by employing a solid strategy they don't leave the outcome of their film to chance especially when millions of dollars are at stake, even over brief periods of time. Your business is a much longer term "project" that requires continuous, long-term investment in your brand reputation. Can you really afford to "wing it"?

Ultimately, the end result of a well-planned strategy is the ability to bring your story to life. It has been proven that people respond far more strongly to a story than they do a sales pitch. Now more than ever, the story you tell (or don't tell) can make or break your bottom line. Snappy one-liners on billboards have crumbled down onto the information highways of the past. People want substance and emotional connection in the form of storytelling to decide which brands they trust and feel the greatest connection with, and therefore will buy from. The consistency and emotional engagement with which you tell your story, from your in-person pitch, to your home page, to your social media, blog, and marketing materials, can either confuse or captivate your audience.

In addition to a persuasive story, the "storyboarding" of your content strategy must be grounded in the WHY of your efforts. There are far too many business owners who have heard that they "should" be on social media but have no idea why. People keep telling them they need a blog but they don't know why. They've heard that they need a "headshot" but have no clue as to what kind or how to put it to good use. What these business owners are missing is a clear strategy for the development and distribution of their words and images; one that will drive them toward their goals, versus scattered in a million directions. Minus a strategy, you are failing to unleash the true potential of all these powerful business tools – social media, websites, blogging, images and more. Without a plan, a tool is just a tool.

That's where your Personal Paparazzi comes in; they zoom out, look at your big brand picture, and help you determine the story that will best connect with your audience, and then help determine the WHY behind all your marketing efforts to tell that story. The power here also lies with using a right combination of words and images to create an experience. If people resonate with the story in its original form, you will be able to later reinforce it at a glance, perhaps even with a tag line or a related image. Case in point: What do you picture when you see the words "Got milk?" An image of someone with a milk mustache, right? The branding behind that particular advertising is so strong that you probably know the product immediately upon either seeing a milk mustache or hearing those iconic two words. After the initial push, you no longer need to always see both elements of the brand message paired together – emotion evoked, mission accomplished, story told.

Points to Ponder:

* What about the impact of your brand story?
* How strong is it?
* Is it evoking emotion and persuading people to buy?
* Are your words and images compelling enough to get someone's attention in the midst of the information "static" so prevalent in our communications today?
* Are you being noticed, heard and remembered?
* Is it easy to tell at a glance what you do, and what value you bring to your customers?
* Are you referable with one click of a Share button on your website or Facebook page?
* Do people have a clear understanding of what you do so they can speak for you and refer business to you?
* What's your brand's version of "Got Milk?"

The key is to tell a story in a way that speaks to your audience. The challenge is being able to do this essentially from inside your business. No matter how clear of a view you think you may have of your business, you are likely dealing with the old "not being able to see the forest for the trees" syndrome. This is simply the reality of being inside your brand, day after day, focusing on the issues right in front you rather than zooming out and seeing the big picture – seeing how others see you. To meet your goals, you need an expert set of outside eyes and the right professional, unbiased advice.

There is a reason why even seasoned professionals in branding and marketing hire outside talent to brand and promote themselves. You might have heard the phrase "You can't read the label from inside the bottle." Your Personal Paparazzi can likely see even more potential in your brand than you may be aware of. They can analyze all aspects of your story and then create the right long term success strategy.

Conclusion

Sales pitches are out. Story is in. Your task now, as a business owner and brand proprietor is to identify the right story that will connect with your audience on an emotional level and make them want to buy. Similar to how filmmakers storyboard a movie in advance, this requires having a clear strategy by which to tell that story. Without a plan that is aligned with your end goals, you may soon find yourself like poor Alice, not caring much where in Wonderland she ends up because she has no idea of where she wants to be.

5

ALL THE WORLD'S A STAGE

"All the world's a stage, And all the men and women merely players; They have their exits and their entrances, And one man in his time plays many parts."

-William Shakespeare

If you think about all the communication platforms available to businesses, that is one crowded stage these days with business owners required to play MANY parts (CEO, CFO, CMO, COO, CIO and more in some cases). And that's just tallying the upper-level management functions. What about being your own accountant, sales person, web designer, spokesperson, graphic designer and social media specialist? Just under the broad category of "social media," today we're talking at least five MAJOR networks alone, with at least one new social media site popping up regularly, all begging for your content to distribute to their users. Now add that to the list of all the other platforms you could (and possibly should) use to get your message out to your audience: website, books, webinars, teleseminars and speeches, marketing collateral, CDs and DVDs, radio and television advertising, billboards, in person networking, press releases, news articles, interviews, email newsletters, blog posts – phew! Are you feeling overwhelmed just thinking of all the things you need to do to keep a high quality professional brand story in front of your audience? On top of that, to truly stay above your competition you need to communicate those words and images across all those platforms innovatively, consistently and with creative continuity so they all integrate into one seamless engaging 3D brand story.

There's also no longer one clear point of entry for your customers to access your brand. At one point in the past a company's website acted like a "hub"; it was the place where people went to read about your products and services, look at visual proof, and ultimately make a buying decision. Now, your audience may first discover you on Twitter, then visit your website, then hear one of your ads on the radio, then bounce back over to Facebook to see what your fans are saying. They may be making their buying decision on any platform at any point, but research shows that most people need many different "touch points"/interactions before they buy from you. That number is growing now more than ever simply because of all the available means by which you can connect with your customers. Businesses must now take into account this new, nonlinear way that brand messages are being received when creating their content and distributing it across all platforms. This also applies to the internal conversations happening within your company. Make sure your social media, marketing, and public relations departments are maintaining an open dialogue to stay aligned on the style, tone, and intent of your message.

It's easy to imagine that many business owners, whether just starting out or decades long veterans, can become overwhelmed by the sheer volume of original content they need to produce, as well as the up-to-date knowledge required of the "rules" on each and every platform. Each one, from individual social media sites to blogging to books, has its own native language and has a unique culture and following, and if you don't have the most current knowledge about what it is and how it works, you may find your content either sticking out like a sore thumb (and in a bad way), or worse, being completely ignored by your audience. For a free download listing current top rules for major social media platforms, visit: http://Personal-Paparazzi.com/SocialMediaTips

Be sure and do your homework before logging on, guns blazing, and making a potentially fatal brand error. You must have the right strategy in place for your brand and for the platforms that are designed to offer you the most engagement.

For example, Facebook tends to put the "social" in social media, with its climate of comfortable casual conversation among friends, inspirational quotes and images and long-winded conversations. Twitter, on the other hand, the ultimate in short form social media communications, sways more toward a younger audience, often peppered with sarcasm and snappy comebacks. Over on Pinterest, when you upload an image from your desktop, you have to edit the URL to send people where you want (i.e. your call to action) or else you've defeated the point of posting the image to elicit action in the viewer. This doesn't mean it's okay to change someone else's URL when you "re-Pin" though – a big "no no" for this particular social media platform.

Remember, there are countless rules just like this, many unspoken but well-known to regular users. It's up to you to determine whether you have the time to invest in learning the rules, paying your employees to learn, or if the best solution for your business is to invest in an outside team of experts. Turn a blind eye and you may find that the world (your customers, your competitors, etc.) has moved on without you.

What often leads to a judgment misstep made by many companies when deciding who should be managing their social media, is delegating it to the wrong person. It may be tempting to ask your teenage niece or hire an affordable intern from the local college to operate your social media accounts. But remember, more than "running" your social media, this person is also now managing and representing your brand message on a very large scale. Each post they create has a noticeable, often widespread, and long-lasting impact on your reputation and people's trust level in your brand. The individual responsible for communicating on your behalf on your Facebook, LinkedIn, Instagram, and other social accounts must be in tune with your company values, brand message, style, tone, and also have the ability to connect with your audience (versus their peers). To put it another way – would you send your teenage niece or intern to close the deal with a potential VIP client?

This is especially true when it comes to the use of humor. Attempts at humor in social media, especially when being funny isn't a normal element of a brand, have gotten more than a few high profile brands into sticky situations.

Remember the Carnival Cruise PR nightmare we discussed earlier and the company's attempts at reputation repair? The piece de resistance to their efforts was a remarkably tone-deaf tweet, promising passengers from one of their doomed (plumbing wise) ships that they, of course, could keep the complimentary bathrobes. This was admittedly an attempt by their social media staff to make light of what was a very distressing and just all around BAD situation for many passengers. But look at the typical age range of cruise ship passengers – older, with many retirees. Was that the right message tone to strike with this audience? Probably not. Comedy is just one example of more nuanced, advanced level content where an even greater level of skill than usual is required to pull it off successfully. Funny for the sake of funny is usually anything but. The key thing, with humor or any other specific tone and style of content, is to ensure that it is native and natural to your brand.

As new platforms for distributing your messages are continuously introduced, and existing ones continue to evolve, it's only going to get more challenging to keep up. But more importantly, the question you have to ask yourself is – do you even want to (or have time to) keep pace with the changing world of brand communications? There is a lot of market research to be done continuously on each platform and if you fall behind or worse, decide to ignore it entirely, your audience will know it and your sales will show it.

While communication vehicles like books, blogging, print advertising, and websites may not change that much over time, something more dynamic like social media will change constantly – and quickly. It comes down to how you want to do business and who you want to do it with. If you want to continue creating content through more traditional means, like yellow page ads, elevator pitches, brochures, and billboards, you can keep doing what you've been doing without worrying about keeping up with new changes. But as we've been saying all along, if this is your choice be ready to potentially see diminishing returns on your investment. If instead you want to reach out to new customers and expand your audience well beyond where it is now, you need to meet them where they are, learn their rules, and integrate your brand message into their world. This new essential function of your business, your Personal Paparazzi, is a great strategy for doing this and doing it well.

Let's look at some general pieces of information that you can use as the foundation of your brand message distribution strategy. First, understand that every single brand communication platform is becoming more and more image centric. This means that when it comes to telling people what it is that you do and why it matters to them, pictures not only speak a thousand words, but can attract a thousand new clients and sell a thousand products. Images are more essential in marketing your message than ever because people are far more likely to remember a picture, than just text. But wait, what about the words? Without a strong call to action – i.e. WORDS – you're just broadcasting a pretty picture to your audience. People might not notice your message without attention-grabbing images, but without a strategically targeted call to action, nobody will know what you want them to do! Think about the lyrics and music of a song. They're fine individually but together, the end result is so much more powerful! Or picture the memorable military recruiting posters depicting Uncle Sam himself, with the call to action – "I want you!" How effective would the words be without the image, and vice versa? Another example is the "Got Milk" advertisements. Without words, you're looking at a person with a milk mustache but have no clue as to why, or what the company wants you to do. The image without words, on the other hand, might not even get your attention in the first place. If you are relying on just your pictures, or just depending on the strength of your copy, you are only telling half of the story.

Having a deliberate, organized content distribution strategy that includes this type of detailed knowledge about various communication platforms is no longer a choice – it has become a must-have tool for the survival and growth of your brand. It has to be systematic, purposeful and clearly support your objectives. At every customer touch point you need to ensure consistent brand behavior, brand impressions, and brand experience. When done well, a clear, consistent content strategy will create a powerful and memorable three-dimensional reflection of your brand, and will help grow your business and make your brand "red carpet ready."

Conclusion

The million-dollar question, of course is: Are you prepared to do this? Do you have the time needed to properly research each brand communication platform, determine which ones are the best fit for your brand, master those, and then invest the daily hours needed to develop and distribute quality content to your audience?

Ignoring the giant pink elephant in the room – the need for quality, consistent content marketing in business – is no longer an option. All the world's a stage, and your brand is either front and center, or invisible in the wings.

6

IT'S SHOWTIME

Which movies get your attention? There is no surefire formula for the popularity or success of a film. Some are flops and some are instant classics. Some box office success is expected, and some is a complete surprise. And often the most unpredictable piece of this is the correlation between the film's budget and its popularity. A titanic-sized budget and great expectations of blockbuster success don't necessarily guarantee big bucks at the box office (of course in the case of the actual film *Titanic*, one of the largest movie budgets in film history did happen to yield historic box office success.) Did the dollars invested single-handedly attract moviegoers and make the film's success a sure thing? Absolutely not, and a similar theory holds true in business.

Big budget doesn't guarantee big success. Think about now defunct retail giants like Blockbuster and Circuit City. Just because you are a well-known, nationwide brand with an established reputation and a product that everyone seems to want doesn't mean you are invincible. You can have the largest, most highly paid marketing think tank on the planet and still fail to capture consumer attention, stay in the spotlight, and keep your sales afloat.

And it's often the hottest brands that have the most to prove (think of the pre-launch excitement that ensues whenever Apple introduces a new "iThing"). On the flip side, people love rooting for the underdog! For every giant that falls, there is a small-unknown brand that seems to come out of nowhere and captivate the public's imagination.

So, whether your brand is a household name or a local "hidden gem", a giant or the little guy, how do you get and keep your audience's interest, especially in today's extremely loud marketing arena? There is so much content constantly getting published, that the digital world as we know it is getting overwhelmed. What can you do to stand out? Before we answer that question, let's look at what stands out to you as a consumer; what makes you stop what you're doing and take notice.

As an example of standing out on a smaller scale, think about your Facebook feed. Whenever you log on, you probably scroll quickly through dozens of posts. As your eyes take in tons of mental snapshots of words, images, and video freeze frames – what actually grabs your attention? What makes you stop scrolling and take a closer look? For most, the answers fall into the categories of: images, friend name recognition, or product/brand name recognition. The third one, by the way, is largely reliant on the quality of content posted by the name brand. You may love a certain product to death but if their social media presence is boring, you're probably not going to stop scrolling. However, when a company constantly posts high quality words and images that are funny, shocking, create an emotional reaction, or are otherwise intriguing, you will most likely stop when you see their name in your feed, thinking, "These guys post the BEST things!"

It's been shown that images of babies and puppies get tons of social media engagement. Babies and puppies make (most) people smile. How can you look at a baby or puppy and NOT smile? This, therefore, means that all brands wishing to get attention on social media should spend all day posting pictures of babies and puppies, right? WRONG! In the world of savvy, experienced social media users, this kind of "pandering" is seen as lame and annoying. Unless, of course, you are in luck and have a related brand – like a dog training center or baby's clothing store. But in all other instances, it will be seen as a gimmick, a momentary attention, costing you points in terms of brand trust and value. As you're deciding what to post, always ask yourself how the content connects to your brand audience and why they would be drawn to it. What do you want to stand for and how will you stand out doing it?

For instance, Oreo has been a tried and trusted brand that has managed to keep their customers' attention for over 100 years. But just because they are "comfort food," does not mean that they haven't found a way to be some of the savviest social marketers out there today. Their Facebook and Twitter pages boast consistently high fan numbers and engagement. They are also quick to keep up with current events, including the infamous "blackout tweet" at a certain high profile football game a few years ago. Oreo impressed many people when the lights went out in the stadium with their simple but effective tweet, containing the words, "You can still dunk in the dark" accompanied by a plain (but professionally done) image of a single Oreo cookie in a spotlight on a dark backdrop. This trusted brand has found a way to represent their long-held core values and mission, while still standing out in today's digital world by using the power of social media to tell a quick and compelling story.

Now, let's step away from social media and look at other brand marketing that grabs your attention. The last time you were driving down a highway, which billboards caught your attention? Why? Ask the same questions about the magazines and newspapers you read, television commercials you watch and advertisements you receive in your mailbox. In the torrent of images and words that confront you every day, from every possible direction – what stands out and makes you stop in your tracks?

Think of the Maxell cassette tape TV commercials and matching print ads, where the person sitting in a living room chair literally has their hair blown back by the power and intensity of the audio recorded on the cassette tape. In mere moments, Maxell found a way to cut through the commercial noise and grab you.

Your customers are surrounded by digital noise every day, so it may be incredibly difficult for them to hear what you have to say. In addition to the impact of the words and images, there are also the emotions that lead people to buy. These emotions can be sorted into two basic categories – fear or happiness. Or in marketing terms, pain or benefit. Pictures of luxury homes and tropical beaches attract attention because they make you dream of the life you could have; they ignite your imagination. On the other hand, marketing messages implying that you could suffer serious consequences if you don't purchase this product or service can make you act out of fear. There's a reason why weight loss is a billion dollar industry in the United States. It's a huge "pain" factor for which everyone is looking for a magic bullet. And if you're the company with the (perceived) solution for a problem like this, people WILL pay attention and pay you money!

Living in the gray area of fear and happiness are: messages that shock you, ones that surprise you, ones that make you go "awww….sooooo cute!"; ones that bring up fond memories from the past, the weird ones that make you do a double take, the tear jerkers, and more. Emotions create a lasting memory in the brain, so when, as a marketer, you can tap into that, you've just grabbed your audience's attention.

When you add images to this, you also engage your viewers' visual memory - a process that allows people to pull associations and past experiences connected with an image. Pictures that create emotional connections will help people relate to your content better. Once it's triggered, it creates a link between your text and the mental image, helping people remember the information you are sharing for a longer period. Yet most businesses do not take advantage of their online visual potential. Their visuals either do not provide enough visual persuasion, are outdated, or simply non-existent. With just a little effort and planning, an eye-catching, interesting, or out of the box image can get you noticed!

The attraction caused by this mental connection between pictures, emotions, text and mental images, hinges on the quality and quantity of the content you create. If you want to sell successfully, you need content. Period. It cannot be an afterthought or a "when I have time" – it needs to be an integral part of your regular work process. Your visual and written content, information about your products, services and programs, is the foundation of your business. Beyond just knowing who you are and what you do, people also need to know the best ways to use your products and services, how to get the most value out of them, and how to select the best ones for their needs. The content needed to do this includes writing and images for press releases, blog posts, product manuals, quick-start guides, instructional videos, workbooks, social media posts, and in-use examples. The greater the volume of words and images that you produce around your products or services, the greater the value you offer to your customers. It's also up to you to educate your customers about that value that they're receiving, and add their satisfied testimonial and stories to your content library. The cycle of content is continuous and contagious. First, your content attracts attention. Next, it educates, entertains, and persuades your audience, converting prospects into clients. Then, you can use success stories like this to gain new clients!

Conclusion

What gets your attention and why, parallels the words and images that make your audience SEE you, especially in the midst of the noisy digital static. The more you can understand the **what** and the **why** of attracting attention, the easier it will be to shine a spotlight on your brand and become a blockbuster success story! Now that you know this – how will you attract attention? Here's a start: Visit our website at:

http://Personal-Paparazzi.com/DiscoveryCall to book your free discovery session to learn how YOUR business either is or is not attracting your audience and how to fix it.

7

BLOCKBUSTER STRATEGIES

We ended the last chapter by asking: How will you attract attention? Here are some specific strategies to attract your audience to your message that you can start using today.

#1: Originality

The independent filmmakers behind the breakout movie "The Blair Witch Project" didn't have a lot of money for marketing. But what they lacked in funds, they made up for in originality and creative thinking. They launched a clever Internet campaign revolving around "missing student filmmakers" who had apparently disappeared into the Pennsylvania woods without a trace. And then there was the myth of the "Blair witch" herself. And then the missing film footage turned up, showing the students, terrorized by an unknown demon, with that "footage" becoming the movie itself. Moviegoers bought it – big time – and flocked to theaters nationwide, forking over their dollars to find out what in the heck really happened to these missing students. Of course there were no missing filmmakers. Call it a hoax, call it clever marketing, but at the very least, it was an original strategy that generated huge attention around their product.

Originality will get you noticed. Whether you are selling a new product or service, an innovative customer service delivery system, or even an existing brand or product, you have the potential to be original in your message or message delivery.

One of the simplest and the most straightforward ways you can separate yourself from your competition is to create original content. Over 80% of all visual content shared, re-pinned, and posted on social media is reused content. So while everyone else simply shares, if you produce your own content it will immediately put you above your competition. Producing original visual content is a great way to increase your credibility and establish yourself as an expert in your industry. Keep your high-quality images fresh and up-to-date, and you will be seen as a business on the leading edge.

A common pitfall for many businesses is using readily available stock images to brand their business. While stock images could work great to support a blog post, or as a background for a witty quote, you should avoid at all costs the use of generic images that can be found anywhere to tell the unique story of your business. Generic is the opposite of unique and your brand image could suffer because of this seemingly innocent marketing choice.

Just like with recycled images, recycled words put your business at a distinct disadvantage. Plug and play or "template" styles of copywriting are certainly an inexpensive way to fill your website, blog, social media, and marketing materials with words. But what does your choice to use generic messaging that could apply to almost any business say about the quality and professionalism of your business?

To learn about other mistakes you may be making in how you "show up" download our free report at:
http://Personal-Paparazzi.com/TopMistakes

Originality in your brand message means really digging in and discovering who you are, what you have to offer your audience, and what makes you unique from your competition. In order to have impact and create an emotional response in your audience, the words that reflect this must be your own and they must be well thought out.

#2: Consistency

Consistency means how often you show up and how you show up to your audience. For instance, if a Hollywood actor works consistently and manages to keep his name in the spotlight (in a good way), he is more likely to get more and more roles. The same is true in business. Think about the commercials that stick with you simply because they seem to ALWAYS be airing!

There's the "Flo" character from Progressive Insurance, the "Can you hear me now?" guy, and the Coca Cola polar bears frolicking on our TV sets every year around Christmas. A consistent brand presence means a profitable business because it's the first one that will be recalled when the need arises.

Consistency will get you noticed, recognized and remembered. It is key in establishing a recognizable brand with strong values. Creating and distributing a consistent visual message across all available platforms will go a long way in making sure you are attracting the right paying clients to your business. Being consistent does not mean being boring and predictable. It doesn't mean that you have to use the same image on every site and in every marketing piece. Rather, it means being coherent, where all parts of your image strategy serve the common goal and support the same message, whether they are used individually or as a series.

Next, take a moment to look at all the words that you currently use to represent your brand message – from your business card to your social media to your website. Now ask yourself, if a client prospect met you and received your business card, then went home and visited your website, and finally logged onto Facebook to "LIKE" your page – would they recognize all those words as part of the same brand? In other words, would they SEE you? Consistency in messaging means maintaining a constant vigilant presence across all your marketing vehicles as well as making sure that what you're saying sounds similar enough in tone, style, and content that people know it's you speaking to them.

Referring back to good ol' Flo from Progressive Insurance, as soon as one of those commercials comes on and she starts to speak, is there any doubt as to which brand she is speaking for? That's the power of brand messaging consistency!

#3: Value

Value, as the business adage goes, means underpromising and overdelivering. When creating any marketing strategies, you should ask yourself: "What value does this create for my customers, followers and prospects?"

For example, one brand that adds value by not just selling to their audience but also educating and informing them is Whole Foods. On the outside it could be considered a healthy grocery store, but this is a brand that goes the extra mile, engaging and educating their audience about the benefits of eating organic and living a healthy life.

To replicate that, you really need to understand your ideal target audience's values.

Points to Ponder:

❊ What are their questions, ideals, goals, and challenges?
❊ What drives them and what matters to them?
❊ What attracts them to you?
❊ Why do they consider and buy your products or services?
❊ What problem(s) does it solve for them?

If you can answer these questions – then you are perfectly aligned to bring value to your client relationships. But you must forget about selling – through your words and images you want to create stories that help educate, motivate and inspire!

Your marketing should not be about you and your company – it should be about your existing and potential clients. Whether you are sharing how-to tips, creating step-by-step tutorials, posting inspirational quotes or documenting how your products and services change lives. If it resonates with your ideal customers, they will share, like and distribute your message without being asked. If you provide value, it will make you more memorable, increase your authority, and position you as an expert. If your followers see that you give more than you sell, you will retain more clients, get more referrals and close more deals.

#4: Shareability

The most powerful content is memorable and shareable. It offers an original message in a simple enough way that others can talk about you and recommend you easily. This means that you have clearly conveyed who you are, what you do, and what makes you stand out consistently throughout all your marketing materials. Your brand message must be easily packaged so it can be easily described.

Never underestimate the power of making content easy to share. You might have created an awesome bold image for your campaign, but if there is no easy way to pin, tweet or share it, it will never become "viral." It happens many times every day. Someone posts an engaging, funny or controversial image, a never-before-seen infographic or a clever quote, and it gets shared. A few times at first, but with every new share it reaches hundreds or even thousands of people. It might even make a news broadcast, or get shared by a celebrity, and then there is no stopping it - it's being tweeted, texted, re-posted and shared on multiple platforms around the globe. Wouldn't you want that kind of exposure for your business?

The bottom line is - if you are in business you want more traffic, more views, more subscribers, more followers and more interactions. If you can get something to go viral on the web, you can get a lot of exposure in a small amount of time without much effort and at a very small investment. The ability to create _and_ share original written and visual content in the right formats and sizes on multiple platforms is what makes your posts into traffic-driving moneymaking machines. Shareability equals profitability.

#5: Storytelling Ability

To sell a movie, you need a powerful story. It's the same in business. In order to sell your product or service, you must attach it to a story that implants an emotional memory of your brand; something that resonates and stays with your raving red carpet fans and cheerleaders. Remember that these individuals can be your most valuable sources of referrals.

Storytelling has always been a powerful way to captivate your prospects and win them over. As discussed earlier, storytelling compels the users to convert more effectively than any other advertising method. Storytelling can be done with one image or call to action that puts your brand message into the right context, with the right mindset and the right elements in a single capture, creating a powerful emotional reaction, getting the points and feelings across quickly and accurately.

Apple has established itself as a forerunner in brand storytelling, attracting attention and igniting imaginations with their inspiring messages of innovation and thinking differently. Their ads are generally instantly recognizable and evoke emotional reactions like inspiration, often just with their iconic visual logo.

Storytelling can also be done with a series of related, coherent images that tell the complete story of your business or describe a single aspect of it (think mini-campaigns or different chapters of your story). Communicating with visuals makes it easier for your audience to absorb and recall later. Provide your customers with a complete visual experience of your business and you will create loyal customers and form long-term relationships.

Every business has stories to tell (business creation stories, customer stories, personal stories, behind the scene stories, products and services stories, etc.). You just need to decide which ones will grab the attention of your target audience and then how to weave them together.

Conclusion

What do these top five strategies for attracting your audience's attention have in common? To maximize your chances of success, it's wise to pair up with someone who has experience implementing them. That's where your Personal Paparazzi comes into play. This new function of your business and mouthpiece of your brand has the power to match the methods of reaching your audience with your end goals. The recurring question, of course, is whether you have the time and expertise to do this yourself or if you'll need to enlist outside professional help to get the job done right.

Takeaways:

❋ Sales pitches are out. Storytelling is in. Your task now, as a business owner and brand proprietor, is to identify the right story that will connect with your audience on an emotional level and make them want to buy.

❋ There is now an undeniable need for quality and consistent content marketing in business. It is no longer an option. All the world's a stage and your brand is either front and center, or invisible in the wings.

❋ Which words and images make your audience SEE you, especially in the midst of the noisy digital static? The more you understand the *what* and the *why* of attracting attention, the easier it will be to shine a spotlight on your own brand, and become a blockbuster success story!

❋ And finally, there are five top strategies for attracting your audience: originality, consistency, value, shareability, and storytelling. Your success with these strategies will be a direct result of the time and expertise you invest in implementing each one.

8

LARGER THAN LIFE

Note: This chapter is specifically written for the unique subset of business owners called "solopreneurs" whose product or service is more of an intangible thing, like knowledge.

"Do the one thing you think you cannot do. Fail at it. Try again. Do better the second time. The only people who never tumble are those who never mount the high wire. This is your moment. Own it."
-Oprah Winfrey

The words in the quote above are certainly inspiring, but let's be honest: The biggest reason for this is that Oprah said those words. She is one of the most high profile examples of an individual who is the face of her brand. Oprah has established herself as a trusted authority when it comes to inspiring people, motivating them, and lifting them up when they are down. Therefore, we trust what she has to say on these subjects and more. Her name, face, and words ARE her business!

Do you sell who you are more so than what you do? Is your "product" intangible, like knowledge and expertise? If your business is branded around YOU, if you are a solopreneur, if you are the product you're selling – this chapter will reveal why having your own Personal Paparazzi is more than an essential function of your business. Since you *are* the business, the stakes are much higher. This level of reputation management through constantly producing high quality content can be the thing that makes or breaks your brand. A company has the luxury of brainstorming who it is and what it stands for as a group, with employees and advisors. But minus a team or a corporate think tank, you are quite literally living inside your message with a limited ability to see the big picture. You need an outside view of your brand so that you can understand what your audience sees, making changes as needed.

Let's take a closer look at "you," the personality behind the profits. Your business positions a human product center stage, with no employees to hide behind. Here are some examples of individuals who can benefit most from the information revealed in this chapter. When it comes to your brand, are you, the individual, "larger than life"?

Life, career and business coaches make up a sizable chunk of this category of individuals who sell information and expertise versus a tangible product. Coaches often rely on name recognition and word of mouth when it comes to selling services that will help people solve challenges and reach their goals. But more often than not, they need additional marketing to reach outside of their regular circles and connect with new customers. Distributing valuable content as part of a Personal Paparazzi reputation strategy can help expand the expert coach's reach and attract more clients.

Are you a speaker or presenter who delivers live presentations with the intent to showcase your expertise, motivate your audience into action, and ideally sell your products in the process? In order to make your brand famous and keep it in the spotlight, you will need to distribute the right words and visual content to your fan base, words and images that sell your message. The same applies to public personas, such as authors, radio and television personalities and others relying on name recognition to make the sale.

What about all the other solopreneurs in business? These are individuals who wear many hats in the business and desperately need someone who can capture the big picture. They rely on their expertise, unique personality, and ability to create solid one-on-one relationships with their clients to make sales and be successful. Think of personal touch services like personal trainers, midwives, counselors, massage therapists and others who sell who they are more so than what they do. They are faced with differenti-ating themselves from hundreds of others in their community who sell the same service. The thing that will get each of them the sale will be who they are as an individual as the face of the brand.

Let's go back to the individuals who, more than selling a product, are selling intangibles like knowledge. Sure, if you're selling a boat, you take photos of boats and write content about boating. Now think of coaches and speakers. What are they selling and how can it be captured by their Personal Paparazzi? They are selling their expertise. Their pitch centers on being an authority in their industry. This immediately differentiates them from the third party sellers, like restaurants. Nobody goes to an Italian restaurant to learn the history and health benefits of a tomato. Instead they go there to eat. To learn more about the nutrition of the foods they eat at that restau-rant, they consult with a nutritionist. The nutritionist is an example of an individual who, in order to establish himself as an expert in his subject matter, absolutely must master every strategy we've talked about so far in this book. He must consistently create content that is original, valuable, shareable and that tells a distinctive story of who he is, what he stands for and what makes his services unique using only quality words and images. Big brands can rely on a quality known product. This nutritionist can only rely on his personal story and knowledge – who he is, his struggles, gifts, and mission. Without this compelling story, his audience has nothing to connect with.

This is true of all the types of individuals highlighted in this chapter. If you are the face of your brand, the ante has just been upped for everything you've learned so far about why you need your own Personal Paparazzi. For instance, when it comes to your "good, bad or ugly" reputation, one per-sonal or professional misstep could have more drastic consequences for a "solopreneur" than a large corporation with many employees to place blame on. It's just you. Think of the difference between singing onstage as part of a large chorus or singing a solo, alone in the center of the stage. When a singer in a chorus misses a note, the audience probably doesn't notice. When a soloist messes up there's nowhere to hide. Similarly, in business, your indi-vidual success is amplified on a large scale. Think of the chef/television per-sonality Paula Deen and how one damaging remark eventually became the downfall of her personal brand. When you are the storefront of the business, every chip in the glass is magnified times a thousand!

At the opposite end of the spectrum, when it comes to growing your business positively, being invisible is not an option. You need to be a non-stop promoter because for most of your audience out of sight means out of mind. It's incredibly important to have a clear, long-term strategy for remaining recognizable, staying in the headlines and newsfeeds and thus in front of your audience.

Once you establish yourself as a trusted authority, people are more likely to buy from you based on reputation alone. Think of legendary actor Robert DeNiro and all his loyal fans that are willing to see any movie he's in, often without even finding out what the movie is about ahead of time. To create this same level of trust and rapport with your audience requires the diligent use of every Personal Paparazzi strategy laid out in this book. The good news is you can do this! Think about how much courage it took for you to (perhaps) leave a stable job and paycheck to forge out on your own, passionate about introducing your unique brand of expertise to the world and sharing your gifts and talents. On top of that you knew that it would be an extra challenge and responsibility to brand yourself versus a tangible product, but nevertheless, you followed through and made yourself the face of your business. We've talked about how Personal Paparazzi is the newest essential function of a business. For you, it is YOUR new responsibility in a business branded around you!

To learn how to market yourself with photography branded around YOU, check out "You Stock: Increase Sales by Branding with Personalized Marketing Photography": http://bit.ly/YouStock

Conclusion

If this message along with everything else in this chapter resonates with you, this is the time for you to take action. If you wait there is a good chance that you will be left behind. If you hesitate you risk failure. After all you've invested in your business, are you willing to risk this? Visit our website at: http://Personal-Paparazzi.com/DiscoveryCall and sign up for your free Discovery Session and find out how to put YOU in the brand spotlight. The stakes are high and the decision is yours. Remember…

"Do the one thing you think you cannot do. Fail at it. Try again. Do better the second time. The only people who never tumble are those who never mount the high wire. This is your moment. Own it."

-Oprah Winfrey

9

THAT'S A WRAP

In 1960, famed film director Federico Fellini took the existing word "paparazzo" (first used in a 1901 travel guide) and gave it new meaning. Fellini was looking for a way to describe the annoying buzz of a mosquito as it darts around its prey, looking for an opportunity to swoop in for its prize. He revealed that the word paparazzo in itself suggested such a buzz, so he applied the term to the main character in the film, a reporter for a gossip magazine on the hunt for a good story. Voila – the word "paparazzi" as we know it today, was coined.

However, one of the things you've seen throughout this book is that when properly harnessed, the "buzz" created by paparazzi can be a good and even necessary thing. More celebrities than ever before have caught onto this and are using the power of the paparazzi to shape the stories they want to tell their fans using a powerful combination of words and images. When used strategically, the power of the paparazzi is the power of publicity, exposure, and reputation management.

The same applies to your business, where "buzz is buzz" and either you're controlling your story, like those story-savvy stars, or someone else (likely your competition) is. It's your choice as to whether you want to harness the power of social media, or if you see it more as an interference and hope it goes away (and p.s. – it won't). Look at what happens when companies tap into this power!

❋ Hertz used a "share it campaign" through Facebook to create awareness about certain discounts and coupons. Almost half of social media users who viewed the coupons shared them with their network.

❋ According to a survey by Harvard Business Review, 21% of "pinners" on the social media site Pinterest have purchased an item after pinning it, repinning it, or liking it.

❋ Fashion house Jimmy Choo used Twitter to locate and target upscale stores that sell their sneakers, and sales increased 33% as a result.

❋ Neiman Marcus's "Thinking Outside of the Bag" campaign on Pinterest, resulted in a 32% increase in pinning activity and 3,000 new followers.

❋ Hotel chain Joie de Vivre harnessed the power of Facebook and Twitter to offer $79 per night deal at its luxury hotels and ended up booking 1,000 rooms that otherwise would have been left vacant.

Unless you learn to use "buzz," like the kind created on social media, to your advantage, you'll never be as big as you can be. In an already noisy digital world, you will just be one voice lost among thousands of others. You will be one lone mosquito in a swarm, desperately trying to reach your target (i.e. customers). The secret is to find a way to give yourself a strategic advantage by controlling your story. Instead of just letting it happen – craft it to your advantage. And as you've learned, the new essential function of your business, one that we've named your Personal Paparazzi can make it a reality. Let's recap what having your own Personal Paparazzi can mean for your business right now.

Stage 1: Finding Out Where You Are

Growing your business is a never-ending journey. No matter where you are, there's always a next level to reach especially when it comes to finding a way to attract attention, earn trust and sales as a result. It all begins with finding out how you're being perceived by your audience now.

Recall our theory of "Good, Bad & Ugly." "Good" means you're being found and generally have a positive reputation. "Bad" means you're being found, but your customers may find more negatives than positives about your business. "Ugly," as it implies, is the worst of all; when it comes to your reputation and visibility in the market place, you might as well not even exist to the people who need your products and services the most. Therefore, the first thing you need to do within this new function of your business is assess your reputation.

Stage 2: Discovering Where You Want to Be

The next stage is learning how to create a vision for your business way down the road by figuring out how you want to be perceived. The key in this step is comparing your brand story now with the brand story that you want your audience to hear and repeat. Remember, if you're not controlling the way your story is told, someone else will tell it for you and you may not always like the results.

Most businesses find themselves looking at a large gap between how their audience currently sees them, and how they want to be perceived.

Stage 3: Bridging the Gap

The secret to telling your story **your way** is to create a constant flow of relevant, quality, current, and engaging content using both words AND images. This applies whether the nature of "the gap" is incorrect information, outdated marketing, or not enough content. Reputation creation and control means constantly fueling the fire; there is no more "one and done" in marketing today. Sure, at one time businesses could use the same slogan for ten years without any negative consequences to their business. But we've since moved way beyond that into a lightning fast digital age. Words and images are literally inundating your audience, constantly and from many platforms. If you're not always generating fresh new content to grab their attention then your business will be seen as outdated.

Figuring out where you are and where you want to be is the easy part compared to the effort it takes to actually bridge that gap with all this fresh new content. Generating that content is where the real work begins. That's where all the strategies you've learned in this book, to constantly create professional content using high quality words and images, come into play. These are the efforts that will truly take you from point A, where you are now, to point B, where you want to be. From the quality of the content to its value to your customers, and your ability to learn and follow the rules of each distribution channel, your ultimate success will lie in the consistent and thorough implementation of your Personal Paparazzi strategies.

And even then, the work doesn't end. Once you've set a plan in place to regularly develop all this content, your next responsibility is monitoring the results and making adjustments as necessary to your audience's rapidly changing tastes and needs. This is a constant cycle: create, monitor, and adjust. Rinse and repeat. With the speed of business today, there is no pause button. You either keep up or fall behind.

Your Choice

"You've gotta ask yourself a question: Do I feel lucky?"
-Clint Eastwood in Dirty Harry

And in business, the question YOU'VE gotta ask yourself is whether being your own Personal Paparazzi is in your zone of genius. Is everything we've described, all the things you need to do to keep up with the speed of change and stay ahead of your competition, the best way you can think of to spend your time? Can you do it well? Is this a skill you have? Keep in mind that being your own publicist, marketer and brand expert takes time away from cultivating business and working in your zone of genius. Or would it be a better choice to stick with what YOU do best, investing your precious time in the passions, skills and wisdoms that you founded your entire business upon?

Because even if you do somehow "make the time" to be your own Personal Paparazzi, remember that quality and results matter. Your audience will be the first to let you know this by choosing to buy your products and services. If you're not connecting with them regularly through quality content, make no mistake, they will notice and if this goes on for a long enough period of time – your bottom line will show it.

If you're being honest about what you know versus what you don't know, you've probably come to realize some vital truths while reading this book.

1. Throwing things at the wall and hoping something sticks is not a strategy for business success. It's a carnival game. Without a clear, out-

come-based plan of action in place with the right people to execute it, you're basically wasting your time. And on top of that, if you're constantly executing blindly without ever assessing results, you'll never know what's actually working. It's all fun and games until the business starts to suffer.

2. Copying other people's strategies does not count as a strategy. What they're doing is being executed based on THEIR goals, not yours. A specific combination of methods and platforms play different parts in every company's plan. Copying just one piece of the puzzle without seeing the whole picture won't get you very far.

3. Going through the motions and producing any old images and words to represent your brand does not count and when it comes to results it does not work. If you want professional results, the simple truth is, you need to hire a professional. Establishing your reputation and making your story heard requires skills that go well beyond taking pretty pictures and throwing words together into snappy sentences. There's a science behind the buzz.

A Recap of Benefits of Having a Personal Paparazzi:

Your Personal Paparazzi can strategically create an abundance of high quality words and images that you need to create your brand story your way.

* They are creative storytellers who fully capture the experience of your products or services.

* Their strategies create strong emotional connections with your audience that makes people feel compelled to buy from you.

* They put you in total control of the story being told to the world about you.

* Your Personal Paparazzi can also assist in the area of damage control when it comes to your reputation, ensuring that there is an abundance of positive publicity to be found about your brand, to bury any negative.

* They are experts who stay on top of all the new and emerging digital platforms, learning the "rules" and staying ahead of the curve, so you don't have to.

* They help you connect with your customers where they are.

Here's the best news yet. You are already ahead of the curve because you invested in this book and took a step towards learning how to stand out in the digital marketplace. Most businesses, including your competitors, do not take the time to adjust their marketing and promotional strategies with the changing times. If you are seriously considering adding Personal Paparazzi as the newest function of your business, you are on the cutting edge. Things that we've talked about like content marketing strategies, harnessing the true power of social media, and tapping into the visual marketing revolution, are just beginning to reach their true potential. Adding a Personal Paparazzi skill set (whether done by you and your team or, more preferably, by outside experts) is your secret to capitalizing on this new way of doing business. This is a brand new, winning strategy that combines reputation management, buzz creation, content creation, and storytelling, and YOU are in the know! And that, as they say in the movies – is a wrap.

Alina Vincent

Alina has viewed the world around her through a creative lens since her childhood in Uzbekistan. She was the girl who came home after a whole day hiking trip with her friends only to shut herself in the darkroom until 3am developing photos of the experience to share with everyone. With her camera constantly in hand, telling stories through images was an early and lasting addiction. When she left her country to go to America to pursue her academic career, an artist friend drew a caricature of Alina next to the Statue of Liberty, camera in hand, ready to visually capture her American dream.

Photography has been her passion and creative outlet, matched only by her education and expertise in math and science. Her analytical background with advanced degrees in physics, computer science and engineering eventually led to a position as an instructional designer, where she used her technical and teaching skills to tell the stories of academic subjects using all the tools at her disposal. One of her tasks was researching and assessing which academic technology should be brought to campus. She learned a valuable lesson therein – the difference between using a new tool for the sake of using it, versus finding the right tools for the problem at hand and using them well.

Another challenge was seamlessly integrating new (and often untested) technologies into customized online training courses based on each university professor's unique needs. This involved evaluating how each professor, subject matter experts in their own right, utilized their course materials, and then helping them design a course structure that told the right story to their students. Her specialized work in this area earned Alina international awards in an annual worldwide competition for "best online course" for an unprecedented four years in a row.

But while these and other honors helped build Alina's career reputation in the worlds of science, technology and academia, they did nothing to help her real passion – photography. When she decided to follow her heart and leave her successful career at the university and open a photography studio, she had to start from scratch. A Google search of her name yielded abundant content chronicling her achievements at the university, but only scarce and scattered "artsy" images she had taken for fun. She did not even have a Facebook page or a website for her new business. As a fledgling professional photographer, she was an unknown. One of the ambitious goals she set for herself in her business was to become the best headshot photographer in the area. She had the skills, the experience, and the expertise, but her existing content and online visual reputation did not support her goals. She was invisible in the digital marketplace among the more established photographers.

While perfecting her craft and taking headshot after headshot after headshot, Alina also worked consistently to establish herself as an expert in her field by producing quality content, social media, blog posts, articles, images and more, to essentially flood the search engines, replacing highlights of her past career that no longer served her present goals. That's when she truly began to realize the power that content marketing, both with words and images, has in building a brand reputation. As she continued to build her business and reach her goals, she started down the path of guiding other businesses in doing the same.

Today, just a couple of years later, Alina has a combined 8,000 Facebook and Twitter followers, has risen above her photography competition, and is consistently producing pictures that have impact. She is a #1 best-selling author with her book "You Stock: Increase Sales by Branding with Personalized Marketing Photography" http://bit.ly/YouStock. She is widely recognized as the best business headshot photographer in Reno and beyond, with clients flying in from all over the country to work with her. In early 2014, she gained entry into an elite group of photographers. She's now

Nevada's only official PH2 Associate Photographer, part of headshot guru Peter Hurley's international referral network. At the time, she was selected out of the almost 5,000 photographers from 102 countries in the coaching network – a selected handful personally recommended by Peter. Having reached her original professional goal, Alina has now set a new course. She found a new calling in helping business owners not only look good in pictures, but also helping them understand the *why* behind their photos and guiding them in representing themselves, their products and services through visual storytelling and visual marketing.

Connect with Alina:
Website: http://AlinaVincentPhotography.com
Facebook: http://www.facebook.com/AlinaVincentPhotography
Twitter: http://twitter.com/AlinaVincent1
LinkedIn: http://www.linkedin.com/in/AlinaVincent/
Pinterest: http://www.pinterest.com/AlinaVincent/
Google+: http://plus.google.com/+AlinaVincent
Instagram: http://instagram.com/AlinaVincent

Christine Whitmarsh

Christine has been a storyteller since a very young age. Friends, neighborhood kids, and even family would spend hours trying to coax her away from her pen and paper, out of the basement, and into the sunlight – but to no avail; the call of the words was far too strong. Short stories became attempts at novels, which branched into writing related extracurricular activities at school such as being editor of newspapers and yearbooks.

The creativity didn't start and end with just words either. She managed to successfully squeeze flute lessons, piano playing, dance, producing plays, and other creative outlets into her studies and of course, her basement writing time. The plotline weaving itself through Christine's seemingly random life became increasingly clear – grasping any and all threads of creative expression and weaving them together into colorful stories.

Then, at the age of sixteen, a personal medical crisis in the form of a dramatically curving spine created a fortuitous detour into the realm of science. Thrust into the intimidating world of doctors, tests, and ultimately, major surgery (with complications), Christine's way of taking control of that world came as a complete surprise to everyone who knew her; rather than going to college to study writing or another creative art, she choose to earn her Bachelor of Science Degree in Nursing. She may not have realized this as her motivation at the time, but in later years, the psychology behind her unexpected career decision became clear. Studying the sciences versus the arts would serve a greater purpose in Christine's life. For the time being though, nursing was the first stop on a winding journey of discovering how to align her true passion with a career path.

Inevitably, the journey quickly veered away from nursing and wound its way back to words, via work in Hollywood as an actress, then screenwriter, director, and producer. In this "world" Christine learned how to combine moving pictures with words to create larger than life stories on the big screen that could capture people's imaginations and deliver messages at the same time.

A career in freelance writing followed, granting the now published and produced writer's entry into storytelling for businesses, brands, and celebrities. As Christine's portfolio of successful words, from website copy and press releases to full fledged books, grew, her mother made the astute observation that she was more of a "business" than a "freelance writer." As a result, in 2003 Christine, Ink. – a full service writing agency – was born. The advantage, she immediately saw, of a company versus a "freelance writer" was the ability to create a solid brand reputation and professional image amongst her fellow business owners. The company went on to tell countless brand stories for individuals and businesses around the world, always driven by providing proven results that clients could take to the bank. Christine, Ink. soon evolved from a one person operation, to a team of professional writers, editors, and support personnel; all collaborating in the creative space to use the power of written content to help businesses and brands control the message they present to their audience.

Today, Christine is once again looking forward to what's coming next in business, working to innovate ahead of the market curve. Christine, Ink.

is currently on the precipice of big changes, all designed to tell bigger stories to a bigger audience than ever before!

Connect with Christine:
Website: http://www.Christine-Ink.com
Facebook: http://www.Facebook.com/TellAGreatStory
Twitter: http://www.Twitter.com/Christine_Ink
LinkedIn: http://www.LinkedIn.com/in/ChristineInk
Google+: http://www.google.com/+ChristineWhitmarsh

REFERENCES

Chapter 3:

http://www.inc.com/news/articles/2010/10/consumers-more-likely-to-use-businesses-active-on-social-media.html

http://www.yola.com/blog/17-small-business-marketing-statistics-that-will-help-you-succeed-online/

http://searchengineland.com/survey-60-of-consumers-more-likely-to-consider-or-contact-businesses-with-images-in-local-search-results-73092

http://bit.ly/150MarketingTrends

Chapter 9:

http://socialmediatoday.com/docmarkting/1897266/top-10-business-success-stories-social-media

http://www.businessinsider.com/pinterest-ipo-revenue-2014-5#!La6Hv

http://socialmediatoday.com/pamdyer/1777136/10-examples-social-media-roi-infographic